D1736687

To Whitney & Aubrey
Little Vets from the start

ISBN-10: 0615542131
ISBN-13: 978-0615542133 (Little Vet)
Copyright © 2010 Lori Hehn. All rights reserved.
Little Vet is a trademark of Lori Hehn of
Hehn Veterinary, PLLC. All rights reserved.
First Printing 2011.

For more information visit us at www.LittleVet.com

Disclaimer: This book should not be used to diagnose
or treat any medical condition in animals.

Albert Einstein Goes to The Vet

A Little Vet™ Book

KITTY LITTER

Story by: Lori J. Hehn, DVM
Pictures by: Don E. Winters

This is my cat Albert Einstein Meowski.

I named him after Albert Einstein who is my favorite scientist!

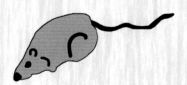

I got Albert from the Humane Society when he was a kitten.

As soon as I saw him, I knew he was the cat for me!

Albert is my best friend.

He depends on me, and I depend on him.

Albert is a happy cat who likes to chase his toy mouse when I toss it for him.

Albert has not been eating well and is feeling "under the weather".

This means he has been feeling sick.

He hasn't wanted to chase his toy mouse,
and he isn't as playful.

Albert started peeing on the floor
instead of going in his litter box.

Mom said Albert had to go to the
veterinary hospital.

Albert tried to hide when he saw his carrier. He knew he had to go to the doctor.

I told him not to be scared, the doctor would make him feel better!

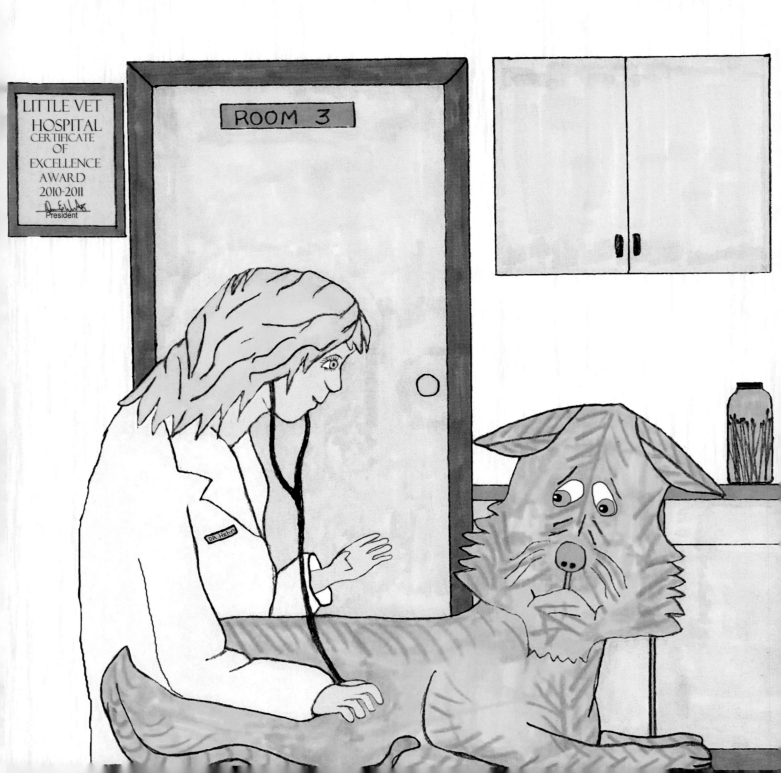

The veterinarian did an examination on Albert.

She listened to his heart and lungs, looked at his eyes, and felt his abdomen.

She collected a urine sample from Albert.

I told her I like science, so she let me help do some tests on his urine.

She did a test called a urinalysis.

She looked at Albert's urine under
the microscope.

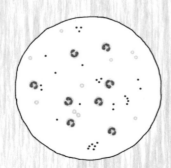

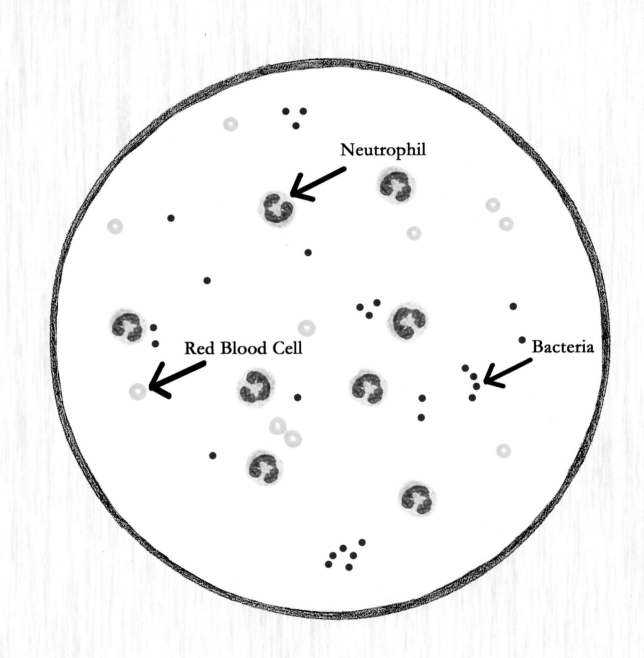

Albert had bacteria and neutrophils in his urine. Neutrophils are white blood cells that eat bacteria.

Bacteria had gotten into Albert's bladder, and that was making him feel sick!

The vet told us this is called a urinary tract infection, and Albert needed to be on antibiotics to kill the bacteria.

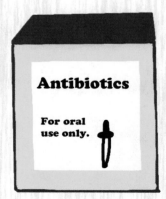

Poor Albert!

He does not like taking his medicine, but I help mom squirt it into his mouth every day.

Open wide Albert!

Albert is feeling much better!

He is playful again and chasing his mouse which makes me happy...

and he stopped peeing on the
floor, which makes mom happy!

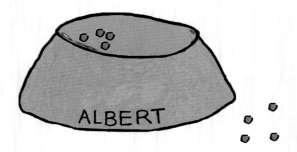

When I grow up, I want to be a veterinarian so I can make pets like Albert feel better when they are sick!

Glossary

Adopt- giving a home to a pet that does not have one. This term is usually in reference to adopting a pet from a shelter or humane society.

Albert Einstein- a famous Nobel Prize winning German physicist of the 20th century who developed the theory of relativity.

Antibiotic- a medication that either inhibits or kills bacteria.

Bacteria- a single-celled organism which does not have a nucleus (prokaryote).

Microscope- an instrument used to see objects that are too small to see with the naked eye.

Neutrophil- a white blood cell often seen in areas of infection or inflammation.

Urine- a liquid waste product of the body that is secreted by the kidneys.

Urinalysis- analyzing or checking the urine for abnormalities. It involves using the microscope to look for cells, bacteria, or crystals.

Veterinarian- animal doctor.

About Little Vet™ Books
A note from the author:

My clients often tell me that when they were little they wanted to be a veterinarian when they grew up. I know my own children love stories about animals and love to pretend that they are veterinarians helping pets. Little Vet™ Books are designed for children who have the desire to learn more about animals and veterinary medicine.

The books in this series each include a different animal species. The books are narrated by the child in the book to whom the animal belongs. The child talks about the responsibilites of caring for his or her pet. The books introduce clinical signs of an illness seen manifesting in the character. The animal goes to the vet to be diagnosed and treated, and new simple medical terms are introduced.

These books are fun for children because they are able to help the vet make a diagnosis and follow a treatment plan, yet the books are simple to understand and fun to read.

I have enjoyed writing this series and hope you and your children will love reading Little Vet™ Books!

30039914R00024

Made in the USA
San Bernardino, CA
21 March 2019